they found a woman's body

mela blust

they found a woman's body ©2020 by **mela blust**. Published in the United States by Vegetarian Alcoholic Press. Not one part of this work may reproduced without expressed written consent from the author. For more information, please contact vegalpress@gmail.com

Cover artwork and design by Christopher Payne • *saltedteeth.com*
Based on a photograph by Clare Welsh

table of contents

something i've learned

birthday cake

blood pact

idolatry

thirteen

doe-eyed as my youth

truth touch hand

mother wound

cut until I see stars

girl with dead father

trespass

fool me twice

dry

girl-shaped thing

dear moon

lies we tell ourselves

everyone knows

ungrateful

rattle

crone

bee sting

teeth

why don't you just leave

sacred union

how to make a mistake

bloodflowers

conjugal

ruins

cosmic alibi

beware the tempest

the burgundy of goodbye

narcissus

the taste is there

famine

come

ripple

the ballet of the adrift

judgment of solomon

tamiami trail

both hearts

every little thing I think about when you choke me

in my lungs

autumn

you move forward

shadows

crumbs

as heavy as water

the other side

american dream

two donkeys and a goat

how our voices change

wishes in the bottom of a well

sad milk

gravitational pull

denial

divine feminine

angel

skinny

hand-me-downs

widow

fluidity

hope

motherhood

oh mother

all the trees have lost their limbs

it rains for days

siren's song

what we learn along the way

waiting

each door

on darkness

lead anywhere home

thin lines

you won't know

fly

spell for home

throwing stones

girl

they found a woman's body

the darkest hopeful song

"I am not in favor of imposing happiness on people. Everyone has his right to bad wine, to his stupidity, and to his dirty fingernails."
-Milan Kundera

something i've learned

is that the smallest sound is a great crashing in the woods at night. it was only the smallest crack of bone. it was only the darkest red and skin peeling away. the sounds were a breath wafting into my skull and the smell – the taste of iron on my tongue. he said never to walk the stones, not to come to the woodshed at night. how could i have known that what i'd find under that stolid single bulb illuminating the darkness would punish me far worse than his leather belt in the noonday sun? i'd always known his hands contained a tearing asunder. how little i knew of his soul until i saw him tear a soft fur coat from sinew; how little i knew of my own when later, i took muted bites of rabbit stew, tears streaming down my face.

birthday cake

once, a man tried to love me, but his love was wrapped in a paper covered with thorns. i let him unwrap *me* instead. there were so many layers of paper. he tried to give me more emptiness, but my dress didn't have any pockets. i tried to love him back, but he couldn't find my name with his lips.

ask me about the winter i spent lying beneath an ocean of blankets, crying jasmine tears that filled the sea of my bedroom. i couldn't come out because i couldn't breathe. see i am full of holes, and somehow still here.

he put nineteen candles on my birthday cake when i was twenty. i still don't know what happened to the year i lost. i blew out the candles, and nothing changed. the next year, i was afraid of the flames. i finally decided the pain of unanswered wishes hurt more than not wishing at all.

ask me if i want to be like this — a black hole sucking all the stars you ever wished on from the sky. i'm sorry i take up so much air.

i don't want cake anymore.

blood pact

we had uttered our canticle,
tied the black ribbon around the sacred box
a weight was lifted but the darkness still whispered: come.
the nights were an adept lover with warm hands
and a cold tongue.

we stole away to the place
of dust motes and ochre
jasmine weaving her scent through the oaks
our bodies contorted in ecstasy
under a godless sky.

the shelves of our feral hearts
stocked with a bountiful supply of wicked pleasures
how we knew the taste of each other's blood,
how algid steel made flesh quiver.
youth, unaware of the spell
of blood.

this was how the darkness bloomed in our irises:
when we opened the box he came out
of the mirror.
after that, it was always breathing
on me.

idolatry

youth is a bleak black ribbon
frayed and fraying and wrapped
around the neck

something dark swallows you
a wisp, a whisper - find the hand
of god

we salt the ache
we wish on wind
we pray for love

hand our hearts to those
who hold
the scythe

thirteen

i lost my milk teeth on tug of war
with my emotions
cut my teeth on silence, on questions
"you're too young to understand"
they said
but the darkness whispered answers to my youthful heart
shadows whispered knowledge
to my teenaged soul
father fills the fridge and
mother fills the dinner plate
but who will fill the heart?
i'm always a little girl, always a little confused
i think about those flowering dogwood tree days
those playhouse tree friend days
and somehow still i'm thirteen
smoking banana peels, skipping school, and climbing a tree to escape
old white man peering into the backyard days
cherry tree in the backyard days
something naïve floating in
my nipples hard in the summer wind
remembering now how much i wanted the attention
i must have deserved every little death
"you're too young to worry about that kind of thing"
mother's voice dies on the breeze
and my youth
cherry flavored pop rock sweet
now tastes of blood like
when i bite my cheek

doe-eyed as my youth

winter comes to take me
 seasonal commodity - honeyed meat still warm
some like their victims
    still

    doe-eyed as my youth
 lips parted
isn't this how the infected
    do it?

   vestal hands shaking,
accept the tempest
    emerge pure

truth touch hand

i am powder fine dust awaiting
fingers, trace these heart cobwebs
away

brush these lines of resignation
fetid stagnation
from the day

crawl into our hole as blood warm beating

meets petal tender mouth
placed upon moon blush cry

quiver with sky
under truth touch hand

slice open star punched backdrop to find
shoes full of doubt
and head full of sand

mother wound

i have a love hate relationship with the night. when the day is done and i find myself alone — not mother, not wife — just naked self and the darkness, she holds me so delicately. all owl call and lavender. we've always been close – like twin flames, like mirrors, so close i inhale her burning breath, she shows me the pieces i don't want to see. in the blanket of darkness something eternally pulls at me, gnaws at me, my mother-wound splaying wide my chest. my delicate songbird ribs, where the heart lies. oh god how i want to sing, but the most distant cry thrums, guttural howl, louder, a pitiful stain on the wind like a lost baby gull, frantic and hungry, a ghost searching desperate shores. my she-child cries feed me feed me feed me

and i am not calm

and i am not sane

and i am not thin

so it won't be bread tonight that passes my lips, but whiskey or wine, because they're the only things not ugly on my hips.

cut until i see stars

each body is a miracle
the generations of women before me
passed down the knowledge of measuring strength with pain

pour wine on the wound, one says
put rouge on the wound, another
instead i try to free the spirit

i could cut until i was thin
i could cut until i see stars
instead, i scrape enough flesh

to be beautiful to men
who want to pour more pain into the urn
it is so full

girl with dead father

my mother has a word
she turns it on her tongue, but spits it out.
i whisper it into the darkness and
it does dance with her loneliness,
although i never say widow out loud.

i search every desolate corner for my title.
i look inside my skin.
the razor finds no noun;
the blood, no language but release.
still i am a hollow thing i cannot name.

i am drowning in adjectives-
glacial, distant, incurable
i breathe so quietly waiting
but no word says "girl with dead father"
and i am mistaken for so many things.

in the first days, months
i will seek until my body shrinks
until my scars become a map
but after years, there is no definition, no destination
and i have settled for ashes.

trespass

porcelain child

      her blush stolen

eternity passes

      in only days

come night

      we drink;

still feel

      eat a decade

like magic

      like a death

bring peace

      this discomfort

fool me twice

i broke a tooth on his sugar

fool me once

sugar highs end in crashes mother said

fool me twice

down came the knife

the sweet song of his fist

to my spine

white glint chipped lying under the bed

later we'd find

it wasn't only me; there was life on this ark

i carried it to safety

through floods, seas of vodka

and storms of percocet he raged

and i sailed deftly, flies with honey, mother said

a finger waggling in my mind's eye

winking at my narrow escape.

dry

hopelessness whispers
at the back of my neck
take a drink, it says
from the ashes of the wreck
despair presses its ragged hand
around the small of my back
gently leading me somewhere
suspiciously hollow and black
promises and laughter
each drop is a beautiful lie
daylight and a mirror
honey, the well's run dry

girl-shaped thing

she wants the body
sleep-warmed and well-timed, humble and midnight-drenched
a home, not like a city.   not like brick or clay—
but a building. sturdy.   all walls and windows.

she craves the teeth, pearlescent and bleached,
a flashy thing to bare or
gnash.
strong enough to bite. a thing of beauty born of
pain.

she knows how it swallows, but spits out the remains.
how it is feral, but timid
how the body lives each day like silk—
threads crossed with threads to make a
girl-shaped thing.

so delicate, so easily torn.
how the mind decides upon resilience
and then pleads
for death.

dear moon

please remember, i never had a chance
i was spinning, dreaming, still drinking
four am brings a hungrier creature than your mouth
thin arms rope around my pale-as-the-sky neck
things get fuzzy when you're drunk, and clearer
in the light of dawn

dear stars
don't tell the secrets you hold from the night before
this pilgrimage inside my flesh was cheap
what does twenty dollars mean to the sky when
the street prays to my feet, following a map of desperation
sucking in the comfort of my sheets
ignoring the blood stains we never washed
souvenirs of my unanswered fertility

dear sky
guide to my spirit journey, wisdom of the ages
guide me home, because .010 is too drunk to drive
and my car is the hollowed shell of a crime scene anyway
where someone kissed the ill-fingered wounds i've dragged around for years
my little fever deaths, running with the wild horses of yesterday
the smell of rot and fertilizer on the pennsylvania wind
a deserved shit-storm less pungent than the hangover i'll marry in the morning,
smelling like the death
of my youth

lies we tell ourselves

you tried to make me so small
stitched me into the tightest of blankets
hiding my curves behind
angles and light
crow's wing hair,
bee stung lips

ashamed of hunger, hungry for joy
denying me so much
denying me sustenance
shiny curls hiding hollowed out cheekbones
later, my throat swallows itself

i'd say it's killing me but
i've been dead for years, hiding inside my stomach
scissor cut and scissor tongue -
lies we tell ourselves about being too much

you couldn't love me because there was so much of me.
so you carved fault lines, breathed white lines
told little white lies.
separated me from god,
made me someone else.

everyone knows

a cut leaves a scar
a thin red line connecting
heart to hand.
go ahead,

trace the lines of how much
i let you love me.
how much
this vessel can hold.

i am rose-petal full now
and moonlight clear
every chipped-glass crack,
a scar so gently loved

not for the searing pain
of the wound,
but for the one
who held the knife.

ungrateful

master gives me a spine
armature made of wire

he weaves around it flesh
and kisses me to life

plants eyes inside a skull
blows a soul into it

and i spend almost forty years
tearing it apart.

rattle

i gather this eroding bone dust
and pour it in front of my feet,
that i have a path to walk on —
as i've always seen blackness
where the ground should be.

how it all fell away the first time the razor
split my skin and
the red trickled out.
how something so tied to losing life could make me feel
so alive.

once, i got into my car and drove to work where
white shirts walked around with scissors cutting words from my tongue
and when i left there was a dead baby mouse
on the passenger seat.
buckle up, i said.

i had held death before; my first husband watched porn
while it poured from between my legs in a hotel bathtub
twice in one year.
i could have picked names but instead they were just blood.
goodbye, i said.

death found me here a lifetime later
told me his name and how lonely it was
but of course
i knew, and i held him close.
i love you, i said.

each way in which the pain and darkness of death touched my life
seemed so graceful,
ink black vultures roosting in the winter pines
above my house;
the dance of waiting.

last week sun glinted off the pavement as i drove my little girl to school.
there was a dead baby deer in the road, a symphony of vultures picking it apart.
as my car rattled toward them, they scattered, one just above us, right above the windshield,
nine-foot wingspan gliding in a silent union with my car, bloody face.
how he recognized me through the glass.

crone

blackest bird of sorrow, i beg,
trembling from the forest of my youth -
sing me the comforts of yesterday
swaddle me in the lightest of blue
a blanket of comfort.

instead, the cawing of danger;
years are dripping through my fingers
the congealed red blood of life exiting my throat in tacit breaths
whispering
goodbye.

breathless old heart forgetting shapes,
tender steps like a graying animal
ready for rest.
borrowing moments because now is fresh and ripe
and tomorrow's plans are only a prayer
to time.

bee sting

when i was a little girl
i cut my porcelain arch
on a piece of green genesee bottle
sharp like
later-hands.
stepped on a bee and cried
not for the sting,
but for the death.

all the years these bones have
carried me
there was nothing like running
from him
enemy-drenched, his steps
and i became the bee
i raged, i raged - a storm of quiet surge
and stung, knowing full well the death
that followed

i found my way to angels then,
they brought me stars and honey
so i could shed my mojave fever.
and my feet were ever tender –
even my missteps.

teeth

there's a winter where my heart should be

death is everywhere

her devotion to us,

and ours to her,

evident.

for years i kept a tooth

in my pocket

turning it over in my hand-

the human it belonged to gone forever

his ashes tossed into the sea.

the ghosts of the ocean

have lost their teeth

tiny white shells turning on the sand

the moon whispers to the tide,

who takes them home.

why don't you just leave?

there's a phenomenon known as trauma bonding
in which you've experienced such profound pain
that someone, or somewhere, becomes a part of you
that you have trouble denying

hometowns hurt in a place that's private
first heartbreak, broken hymen
look inside the ache
a butterfly lands on a pile of shit because shit
grows beautiful things

it hurts in a place that's public
a yearbook's "most likely" embarrassment
it's ok to want to go home sometimes
unless home is no longer home

when they've forgotten your ghost,
ask yourself why you feel love for a place
that doesn't even see you
ask yourself why you feel love for a place
that would cut you down if it did.

sacred union

you were/and were not my

preoccupied assailant

huddled me in a corner/empty juice box

gave me something to cry about

first and ten blaring over the

rabbit ears/and you were gone again

leaving me in shallow water/ending with

sign on the dotted line

how to make a mistake

   bitter dust moth he was coming round
put on gloves to touch because:
  evidence
fought me arms round tight
fleck of sunlight
whitewashed fencepost i am
   bent over like a maid
catch me in a whirlwind with
 panties agape; later,
we watch particles
   land on foreign tendrils of hair
 control panel beeps
    recording, recording
i only bit once
   spit twice

bloodflowers

from the prison of skin;
a bitter pill.
unexpected bloodflowers
bursting the soil.

backwards/a time when we
wrested joy from the wind
now the knife,
a love-shaped gift.

conjugal

glass love attached a stretched beside

should my bones rope through.

hope dangles a lick of hands;

you protest the landscape of my next heart.

we've waded through sustenance

tornado pried from the whisper of drowning.

how we climb the night's ribs to see the

dark jury

out of every rose came a flood and that storm,

the ember of open mouths.

the god-shape behind lips.

ruins

here lies innocence
always the thorn in your side
lascivious uncertainty
swallowing her pride
to tender clockwork within
a fond farewell you bade
greetings, dust and cinder
these ruins you have made
lapping at your shadow
if only for just a taste
gestures lie unnoticed
worship goes to waste
upon this rag doll stitchery
your actions make their assault
i was only eager to a point
but loyal to a fault

cosmic alibi

you left a spot called distance

your mind keeps questioning still

but summer never lasts forever

and time isn't mine to kill

day and night meld into one

your recycled alibi

you specialize in wasted breath

i, in getting high.

beware the tempest

this gin addled night

how one set of words

can crack the dawn

any soul still clutching

a lowball glass

knows the rust growing over

these ventricle windows

the hands of the clock

their own gentle tombstone

the ochre of your skin was home

until it wasn't

the burgundy of goodbye

he begged these thighs like you would speak in tongues at a revival to prove that you'd felt the spirit. he prayed to these teenage dreams and i woke up in sunlight, the cracked sidewalk vomiting hyacinths. we drank once, ending the night with cheap words and stolen breaths outside his apartment while his wife slept inside. the wind blew his cigarette smoke in my eyes, giving me something to cry about. we prayed for forgiveness under a dead moon and hallelujah tears sailed down his cheeks. the tongue that slaughtered virginity, the middle child, the blue-collar working man apparition, showing up with a hard on, wandering the hallway with a scythe. waiting to see the ochre colored seventies shag carpet bloom with the burgundy of goodbye.

narcissus

there is no heat
from your mouth anymore- a
cold, dark longing

when you exhale
a ghost flies from behind
your tongue

we share a pillow/choking
on your hair
an appropriate metaphor for

your vanity; my sanctity
my mouth stretched open wide,
receives your communion

the taste is there

wait for the wires to come down
burn us out of the corner
i don't always have
to be brave.

i put myself into a container
that you can understand.
you zip and unzip me
past the point of wrong.

we use words because
we have no sex
although the taste
is there.

your turn to pull
the rope is fraying
turn to the last page because
i want us to break.

famine

if my body was a red red river
you didn't dip a finger to test
you drank, you bathed
you soaked until nourished and i
i felt the tributary narrowing.

if my body was a temple you did not pray
you sinned, you begged
you fell upon your knees to worship and i
i let you tithe your way
to heaven.

if my body was a waiting mouth
you did not kiss
but breathed in, swallowed
sucked until everything that was once i
was now you, and you loved you best.

if there was a line where you ended and i began
you blurred it, you smeared it
your anger rubbed my soul quiescent and i
i only wanted to feed you but
i forgot to eat

come

taste the wretched honey of my sins

wrench the last breath from

the poverty of my lungs

how many times have i been on my knees

praying for the next delicious theft

see these hands

built this shrine so that you could worship

a come-hither demon.

the lie we think of as love.

ripple

your core/bone/underlayment

holding up the model, hair and skin

your skeleton/frame/dust/marrow

keeping all the secrets in

your heart/breath/function/sex

tethering me to your side

your strength/wean/glance/empty

casting away the tide

the ballet of the adrift

flames dance in your irises, the ballet of the adrift

the gentle melody of the asunder

each note lifts a limb. not weightless, not empty.

your heart a harp's note – full, unquiet. not devoid of beauty.

the sparrow song of the weary. star-shorn;

how the notes carry on a breeze

gentle, moving forward into an uncertain twilight.

a series of steps,

like footprints erased by the sea.

the passion is rusting on the vine

listen - do you feel the wind of wanting

so deep in your bones?

how the frets are played for change, how the skin begs.

how do we go on from here, this yearning?

how the water warms with touch, how the touch fades from view

we've gone so far to not heed this call.

like the tide plays to the moon – a lover, left behind but still aching

flicks a gentle wrist, and the sea responds.

i keep feeling you in my bones

the golden clock-tick of moments past – weary sigh of keys long played

you live in my marrow, silent in a hollow place,

furtive and curtailed, but breathing.

a thing of cello-cried sorrow, wind-worn and sonder you call—

and i don't respond

judgment of solomon

you walk me to your room,
hostage to my jewel-soaked eyes
somewhere in that scarlet chamber
i lose my god costume
and we never find your tongue

i float into the cerulean dusk
your soundtrack still reverberating in my sternum
you call and my hand calcifies staring at the number
a thousand arms couldn't hold me back from the acid
of your devil's kiss

how the swift raven of your taxidermied heart
flies into my mouth
the dissonance between intention
and action
cleaves me in two

half for me, half for you

tamiami trail

rust breath/liquor sweet

missing front teeth/french kiss street

colored paper/wrap you please

birthday gift/offering to trees

both hearts

looking back/waters calmed
under blue-strung breath
your white knight iron-lung
stole dusk with such breadth.

whiskey drained/word-drowned
each night flag-waved
the surrender of this adjunct
bad dream/war-craved

cocaine bluegrass/bedtime secrets
stomach lining/death-howl
never-breath good night
both hearts/thrown towel

every little thing I think about when you choke me

a sea foam green treasure trove in an underwater lagoon, glittering bubbles rising to the surface/crystalline quietude/waves breaking violently against a blinding white shore/a dripping faucet that slowly drains the well/broken glass christmas ornament on wood floors/a rocking horse still moving but no one is in the room/a phone ringing in an unknown room/a voice in the night that wakes you from dreams/a car accident on your street with a bag lying beside the car/papers that are due/a kitten sleeping on a sunny windowsill.

your hands around my neck.

in my lungs

i welcomed your angry hands
because anger
always lived in my lungs.

i romanticized all the little deaths
because everything inside me
was already rotting.

i remember vividly the first time i realized
that storms didn't scare me –
came from inside me.

how i raged, gifted you the bomb
watched as the ash consumed you
how beauty and pain were the same.

autumn

i waited by the shadow of your mouth
buried under a deep, pensive blanket

but you were a petal already fallen
from a flower i could not name

your language of unfinished breath
a scythe rusting in the field

the somehow echo of us
a pull-cord broken at the light

you move forward

to place a pendant on a gravestone.
i want to tell you a story about the human heart
but instead i have to tell you a story about a hole
where the heart used to live.

i thought we had agreed to stop being machines
but i've watched you become something made of spare parts
a bottle of wine, a pill, other, forgotten things, anything, really,
if it fills up the space i used to occupy.

we promised once that we wouldn't drift apart this way
now promises are nothing but echoes
clawing at the walls of the place where you used to be
alive.

shadows

lay with me tonight,

for who knows what the morrow may bring.

the birds that bestow the dawn

so seldom happiness sing.

our lamp that lights the dusk

extinguished till the morn,

tongues taste paradise.

fog restlessly born.

wandering like ghosts

these things we leave unspoken,

while you explore my desolate wonderland,

my love lays alone and broken.

and when sunshine is born,

casting shadows from the trees,

my pleasure melds with sorrow.

brings me to my knees.

crumbs

oh how my hand can just lie at my side
as though it knows not what it's done
and can blindly wash the other
and pretend there's only one.

how your heart can staunch the bleeding
and lend apology
to the issuer of such grandiose wounds...
instigator of misery.

why did the glass just shatter,
and leave us here to twiddle our thumbs?
my god, how man can feast on love
while we subsist on crumbs.

oh how our eyes can meet again,
and to our wilted gardens tend.
with tattered souls, we shift from lovers
into weary friends.

as heavy as water

mere dust shadow|cascade of discourse

tired caveat|kicking dead horse

drowning perfume|mean girl blues

mud front teeth|paper weight shoes

dirty bathroom ode|truth is obtuse

rusty fire escape|loop the quiet noose

the other side

the grass

isn't always greener

i know this

deep inside

i am disappointed

now

that i'm on the other

side

american dream

i can't hold you with this

american dream

the knuckles are scraped

the thighs are bruised

and i'm afraid of everything

that moves

i can't look into a mirror anymore

without repeating

what it already knows

it doesn't want me/

i am not home in this skin

if i break it

will there be seven years of bad luck?

add it to my tab

i can't hold you up with this

american dream

in america

the weight of you

will be the death of me

two donkeys and a goat

women are worth so much;
come with so much
everyone knows the hero
gets the girl, gets the dowry
two donkeys and a goat
and a warm wet place to bury

your sorrow
act now; a hot meal is worth so much
a warm breast: a place to
repair your inner child
and only for the price
of her childhood dreams

how our voices change

we were only children then, our laughing

feet coated in sand, running down the sugar

white shore.

we used to throw ourselves against the dunes,

then stand up and watch the dusting of snowy sand

float away

like our dreams have now that we are

thirty something, bored, and apathetic.

our laughter used to dance like butterflies, now

it is heavy like the waves.

wishes in the bottom of a well

turning, unturning

there is a moth where the light

  should be

  and no light

i'm bleeding, this moon is the cycle

let it ruin to rot, never turned

    to embryo

wishes are pennies

    we never threw

pennies are arms

     with no hands

i couldn't throw when the well

was empty

god doesn't dance

  without light

light doesn't pray

  without solace

ballet can't be seen

   in the darkness

my cave is nightlight lit, whisper-sweet

     and dances alone

love can't try to be anything other

    than love

sad milk

pluto has a heart shaped sea on its surface

filled with poisonous ice

whatever is burning in a throat is

less fatal.

but there is no way to tell someone

the way the lines lick at a vulgar destiny.

the way you can see right through to the core;

can pluck the last tragic fruit

from the rotting vine

and still it will tempt another.

trains can depart and arrive and be late

and spill passengers onto asphalt like a sad milk

but your voice may never find a way inside the cold chamber of desire.

whatever you try to walk off

escapes the predatory stare

don't they dedicate themselves to the illusion,

and you've no choice but to float your tongue?

gravitational pull

the gravity of a black hole is so strong
that nothing can escape, not even light
i have prayed to this apogee but it falls
into your silent darkness

i love hate love hate love hate how we orbit each other's tongues
each rebel yell code for pillow talk;
how we fuck each other whether clothed
or naked

see i have lived long enough to perceive
the most delicate subterfuge
lived long enough to try
stockholm syndrome on for size

let me tell you how i can flirt with this perigee
silver tongued and evasive;
stardust that gets too close to a black hole gets sucked in
and never escapes

denial

the teeth push the tongue to its destination and
   this is how lies are born.

i can feel the sound of skin peeling away from bone
as saccharin words emerge from my halcyon mouth.
flies with honey, my mother always called it.

  like catching a fish,
then ripping the silvery hook from the lip and
  tossing it back to the waves.
  it was never there.

  the next morning i want to hate you, but
instead i bring you a plate of eggs.

who is this robot conspirator?
did she laugh when she heard the skin peel away?

we can fool ourselves
  for quite some time.

divine feminine

princess television is warping again

each portal, another hand reaching for flesh-bits.

screams measured in emerald

the fahrenheit of her existence.

diamond drops frozen to the branches

of her tightly wound hours.

extends pearlescent eyelashes as payment,

trade rate cumulative,

glass ceiling wrist slit.

angel

  each hollow
   pay homage
    trace where the line

  could you feather, could you wing,
  in abeyance to your spine?

  what cracks the sun
   from dream to dawn
    to fingertips again

  the kingdom of your solitude
  to lick the red wound clean?

skinny

at first she hid from the pain

each pound a layer of discomfort lost:

how she concealed

    the heart

her weapon fingers

stabbed at the weight

we only kill

    what we know

sometimes even beautiful

the thinnest of beasts

the taste of skinny

her only   sustenance

when they come for the heart

say the name: mother

all other names have been

purged

hand-me-downs

each hand takes on a burden

flick my wrist as the earth turns

another rotation.

she waits behind the glass

we've already shattered;

fragments of my electric youth we cut ourselves on

so radiant it could kill

us both.

the garden of discontent grows tall,

this summer i imagine the blooms

will rot right off the vine as months go by

and i don't come home.

her eyes grow as narrow as the sustenance

i allow myself, as the stars neither of us have

in that sky.

i am not so different from her.

widow

we picked up the pieces of her
 gentle drowning
delicate edges frayed by
clocks ticking away the moments
days fingered her soul like skeletal hands
  turned into days, into
the queen anne's lace of empty bottles
 the sigh of time passing/as soft as each
glass breath she took/each breath
 one step further away from disease's womb

she cries the dawn/her tears are
 dahlias that break the surface of
a barren landscape
her mouth flies through wine on
  wings of necessity
she exhales and her life
is dust floating in a sunray; beautiful,
yet remaining
   a thing of dust

between two sparrow's eyes
she wanders/gathering kindling because
  something has to burn
body still warm, heart still
stuck somewhere in a swan's ribcage.

fluidity

something spooked a flock of blackbirds
in a sleeping cornfield
hundreds of tiny shapes fluttering
moving as one
in a graceful sort of panic.
and then they settled
back down into
a comfortable place.

how i wish that i, too, could experience
panic
in a graceful manner,
that fear could elicit fluidity –
a dance, and not a misstep.
how i wish that i, too, could
fall gently
back into place.

hope

it is all the same
   concept

allowing children to grow up,
     hearts in jars

   clocks ticking; scraps of paper
with hopeful telephone numbers

holding hands next to a
  hospital bed

shaving before a date,
even leaving your door unlocked at night
  is a kind of hope

  we are all guilty
    of.

motherhood

crumpled and matted before me,

an offering no one

ever asks for

melding with the road, wet

and wetter as

my tears fall

how silent it can be even with

cars rushing by

casting wariness aside for compassion

as i tenderly scoop the only days old fawn

from the pavement

its crushed limbs dangling across

my motherly arms

and i put someone's angel

delicately into

the soft meadow grass

as though it never left.

oh mother

you can't understand this kind of hunger
the unmothered sailing through crowds like ghosts
fishing for the next high
flesh of my flesh, blood of my blood
wine can't wear this wound down;
a band aid stuck to a scab
on the heart.

oh mother, the childlike god of sacrifice
tell us it won't hurt
read us something righteous
to curb worms tunneling into our thoughts
our prayers are balanced on the edge of a razor blade
under the floor
of our church.

they're handing out new tongues
to replace the ones that burned
with truth
no more dirty words
wash your mouth out
reading corinthians while
our noses delicately bleed.

all the trees have lost their limbs

you were the child who dared the moon

to drag your new body to the map of something real.

like the bones of the one-hundred-year wood where we played

as children

now the bones are our souls in a

new place, old feast

your eyes on our forested hearts.

how burdened we are with tradition

breathing in and out of the present

ideas you aren't supposed to think

are only sixteen once.

remember your wild, broken laugh

we said goodbye a hundred times before we ever said

hello new day same sun new morning

dew split the rays of light on the grass-

fed absence of meaning in the chasm between

what we left in our yesterday

and the alarm you have come to rely on.

clock wings of amber turning

over the leaves;

the leave of absence you took when all was young and full of promise

i held a dust mote in a ray of sun in my hand

and when i closed my fingers i swear to god there was nothing

to fear

but my hands are empty now like the bank account you pray to and

at the five-o clock whistle you drop to your knees

like a soldier lined up to witness

the shocks of a pornographic sadness

i swore i'd never beg but god is a hungry mouth

and we are all going to be swallowed

whole.

it rains for days

it rains for days

for weeks

you don't come out of your room,

you don't come out of your skin

the walls seep;

windows rattle a tune you can no longer remember

reminiscent of darkness,

of wet, of acrid

the chasm you fall into, a thousand miles deep

when you finally admit the demons you were facing

were all inside

of you.

siren's song

lure you with breadcrumb hips and

star stung eyes

into my damp forest,

ripe with siren's song

descended from ancient bloodlines

soft cottontail fur and

disturbed earth

where thin slivers of desire

fold in and over on themselves

to become the knife of my lust

where sinew joins with bone and

smashes itself against similar softness

where diamond eyes

are mirrors

and limbs twist into snakes

and then, only then

do i decide

whether i am predator

or prey

what we learn along the way

these arms are still home/these legs don't work
the way they used to when
they'd walk twenty blocks to drown out a thirst/
now you're a hunger
that feeds off of the lining of my
heart; my heart a fresh red like
placenta.

but all is full.
we never actually   cut the cord.
things are sinking but   things are surfacing.
they say growth is pain
i am five feet two
what will i be when you stop?

waiting

eyes wide open this evening floating
on a honey-cried moonbeam, remembering how
i used to let the stars sing me to sleep
now they call to me
shiny lures dangling in the whiskey sky i
open wide to drink, to dream/
sometimes to forget
that i'm
a thousand raging tears trapped in a raindrop.

when will the tension be too much? when
does it burst, exploding into the nether?
when will my star-coated fingers reach down,
scrape the dredges of my soul, and hold them out,
bleeding, as an offering
to god?

each door

hear this;

dissolve   almost as though

you were home

question: is this love,

what they spoke of?

a product, wrapped in paper

and sold

but the right thing

at the wrong time

is still   wrong.

what stands in the way

is you.   all that needs

to heal.

the wound does not define,

only resides.

you will be   instrumental

purpose speaks with intention

each door, each step

brings closer to

something brighter, shines

meet the light.

on darkness

what can define it/does it define
you?
you decide

stars decide   where to shine
when to die
they know/the time.

you may call it yours
even as it owns you
because it does/own you

but deny it/ spend a lifetime longing
for something you cannot even
describe.

know this: if darkness is inside you,
(and it is)
you don't have to let it win
but lie in it/
name it.

lead anywhere home

the way she loves is
the way you would pray to clouds.
but they always   float away.

settle these roads - i know
they don't lead anywhere home.
she turns the wheel.

you know how you can feel
a storm is near?
the thunder – actually your heart.

thin lines

think about what they take
yes, but
think about how you let them
this is how we are raised
a temple of loneliness praying to
temptation

think about what is gained
oh, but think about
what has been lost
if you are a dead butterfly in a jar
at least you were pretty enough
to collect

now, dream about what comes next
oh, now, but
don't dream too far
it is the thin lines that separate
what we were from
what we have become

you won't know

you won't know when the ghost slips out of you
whether with a bang　　or just a breath
a step forward　　or a leap
when the smoke clears
and you find yourself somewhere unknown

you won't know when you've changed
 just enough to leave behind
pieces of yourself
crumbs to find your way home
when home shifts from comfortable to weary

you pack your things
and go quietly into the night
the compass points north but
　　　everything feels south

you won't know why the song
　your heart sings
sounds so faded
like the beat of a faraway drum

you'll follow the river to somewhere new
where you can lie your head on a different pillow;
count your breaths
and start again.

fly

time put a bird in my mouth
and told me it couldn't fly
the bird sat breathing
my lungs filled with feathers
and a voice came from inside
shameful, shameful
close your wings

man came like a wave and kissed me
sea of desire drowning the bird
how i've wanted this ocean,
every drop a delicious burden.
the bird was crying:
painful, painful
breaking these wings

god came to heal the bird
asked me why it couldn't fly
my heart was a pearl
i held out my shaky hand
clenched fist opening to the wind,
feathers floating up into the ether
freedom, freedom
spread these wings

spell for home

it's stagnant here sister, this collection of shape-shifting walls. this staging of paint and glass with a choke hold on your breast.

do you remember when you were all wave crests and luminous jewels? how the moon syruped your back, coated you like honey and you sang its song till dawn? stumbling home star-drunk with lullabies on your tongue? don't lose sight of this one sacred vessel. force your legs forward, your feet to find forest. tiny birds, bellflowers are waiting for the blessing of your petal tender steps. remember home.

your blood perfume

will always howl to the fecund moon;

your orchid limbs

playing at the serenity of dance

the streetlights clutch their pearls

in your presence

burning coyly through the flame of desire

choke back the burgundy curtains

the wind will carry you into the night

as light as a raven's feather.

and you will be home.

throwing stones

girls are a scrap of lace looped through bloody fingers,
crawling from our graves of quietude
fragments of bone, crimson stains, and dirty feet
unearthed ivory corpse as gentle as piano key
gently clutching wisps of vulgar memories

at dark we pray for crow's feet
tired of smelling strange sheets
never get to go to bed sweet

prayers come from the jagged wound of a rouged mouth
girls breathe in and feed from the lightlessness of your soul
whatever goes in, comes out.
we aren't dolls, you know
we aren't made of glass

girl,

whisper. your voice is too loud girl speak up no one can hear you girl change you are so behind these times girl stop changing we can't keep up girl go home you are where you shouldn't be dark alley lit bar same street old town girl come out we need your service your voice your body your loving your sex your mothering your care girl amp up you are needed girl calm down you're too this you're too that you're too much girl shape yourself into things you never wanted to fit into girl stay in this stasis this constant this uprising girl voice girl shape girl never girl thing just girl do what they want never what the girl wants and now girl just listen girl fire the cannon girl run we're not safe

girl go now just stand make a stand.

girl.

this home is too tight.

on the other side of this chrysalis you're a butterfly.

they found a woman's body

i called my mother with death upon my heart/lips
silence too loud for sound
i had to tell her about the forest she was walking in
how

they found a woman's body

every singular moment ached into that one sentence.
hasn't it always?

they found a woman's body
laying at the cracked steps of tomorrow

shards of grass protecting her
a smoke bomb tear gas flash bang
away from whatever comes next

the sun and the moon and the earth make a sound
we can't hear it because we aren't collectively
listening

but if you graze your fingertips across the tops of grain
you will feel her breathing

they'll pull aside the curtain one day; they'll tear it all down

and when every willing and able soul steps forward with light in their hearts
desperate to be fed and
aching for love,

they'll find

a woman's
body.

the darkest hopeful song

we are riots in long deserted streets

raging oceans trapped in globes

lips assaulting faces

nipples – branches growing from

invasive trees

fingers weaving a tapestry

from threads dying to turn themselves inside out

eyes always selling something

a smile, a weapon, heat

hoping to break free from the loving hands

of our captors

as our children spread joy among desolation

our hearts are filled with the scripture of survival

and our bodies are notes

of the darkest hopeful song

acknowledgments

the author wishes to express gratitude to the following publications in which versions of these poems originally appeared

something I've learned – lily poetry review

blood pact – tilde literary journal

idolatry – coffin bell journal

thirteen – coffin bell journal

trespass – the magnolia review

dry – the rye whiskey review

lies we tell ourselves – southern florida poetry journal

everyone knows – Connecticut river review

rattle – the sierra nevada review

teeth – eunoia review

how to make a mistake – the magnolia review

bloodflowers – rhythm & bones dark marrow

ripple – inked in thirds

autumn – southern florida poetry journal

as heavy as water – the magnolia review

two donkeys and a goat – collective unrest

wishes in the bottom of a well – the amethyst review

denial – inked in thirds

fluidity – del marva review

hope – califragile

motherhood – southern florida poetry journal

oh mother – heretics, lovers, and madmen

all the trees have lost their limbs – santa clara review

thin lines – rhythm & bones lit

you won't know – rhythm & bones lit

girl – yes poetry

the darkest hopeful song – 2020 Beat Gen Anthology

www.ingramcontent.com/pod-product-compliance
Lightning Source LLC
Chambersburg PA
CBHW022014120526
44592CB00034B/848